Sweetness of Salt

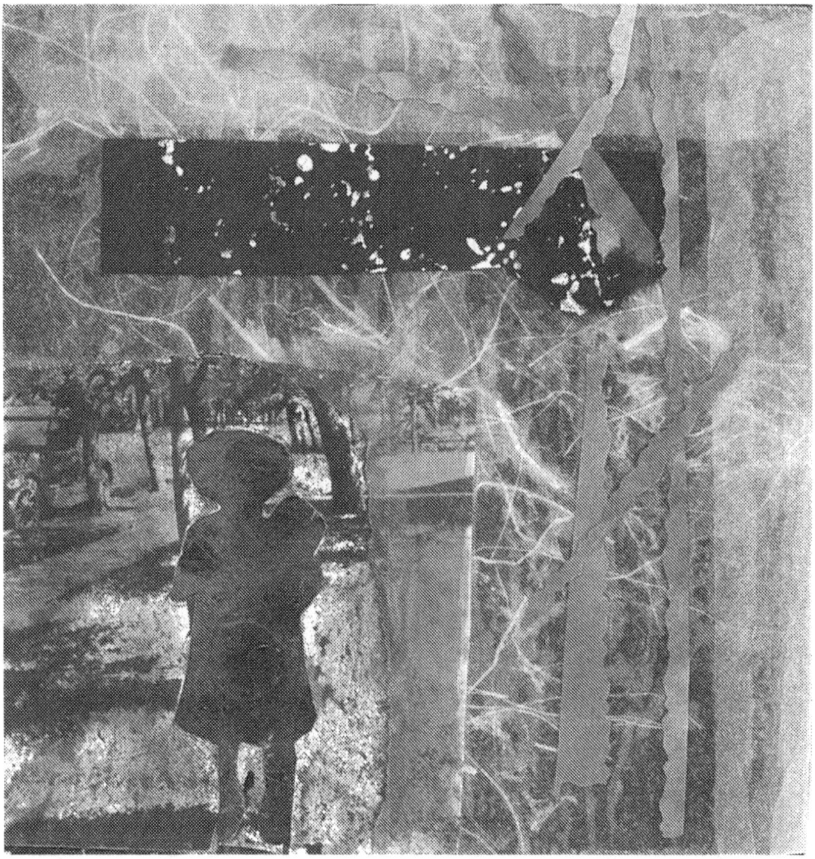

MK Ajay

Plain View Press
P. O. 42255
Austin, TX 78704

plainviewpress.net
sb@plainviewpress.net
1-512-441-2452

Copyright MK Ajay, 2007. All rights reserved.
ISBN: 978-1-891386-90-9
Library of Congress Number: 2007936803

Cover art: CB Follett, detail from *Dreamscape VIII*, ©, 2006 a two-sided piece 18" x 18." Website: http://members.aol.com/Runes

Acknowledgements are due to editors of the following publications in which some of these poems first appeared:

Indian Literature [National Academy of Letters, New Delhi, India]: 'Leaves', 'Drift song', 'When I woke up' and 'Tracing this city's mythology'; *Muse India* [Secunderabad, India]: 'War against terror', 'Time's prisoner', 'Word from the kingfisher' and 'Shadow that became rains'; *Ampersand Poetry Journal* [Austin, Texas, USA]: 'Bishop's forest trail', 'Tamarind tree' and 'Witnessing creation'; *Kavya Bharati* [Study Centre for Indian Literature and English Translations, American College, Madurai, India]: 'Walking to the duck pond', 'Flame-of-the-forest, Beypore' and 'Eye'; *Montreal Serai* [Montreal, Canada]: 'At Malibu pub, Kuantan beach' and 'Malacca'; *Ygdrasil* [Ontario, Canada]: 'At Malibu pub, Kuantan beach '; *Poems Niederngasse* [Zurich, Switzerland]: 'Onset, at Kozhikode'.

Thanks are due to AJ Thomas and Tabish Khair for their encouragement and kind attention to my craft, and to Susan Bright and Plain View Press for making this book possible. I am grateful to CB (Lynn) Follett for her lovely painting which appears on the cover page.

As always, my gratitude to Lakshmy and to my bundle of joy, Satvika.

In memory of Achamma

Contents

Leaves	7
Shadow That Became Rains	8
Witnessing Creation	9
Face On Mirror	11
I Dreamt Of Grandfather Last Night	12
Time's Prisoner	13
Tamarind Tree	16
Walking To the Duck Pond	16
Flame-Of-the-Forest, Beypore	18
Moulded Vessels	21
War Against Terror	23
Tracing This City's Mythology	24
Childhood	25
An Indian In Manhattan	28
At Malibu Pub, Kuantan Beach	33
Definitions	38
Drift Song	40
Bishop's Forest Trail	41
Lobby, Intercontinental Barclay Hotel, NY	43
Ixora	44
Near the Creek	45
Playing With Wind-Goddess	47
Eye	49
Dialogue	50
Psychoanalyst	52
Word From Kingfisher	55
Metamorphosis	56
Exiting a Subway Station, 34th Street	57
Onset, At Kozhikode	58
Picking Yellow Beads	59
Malacca	61
Changing Colours At Dawn (Fraser's Hill)	63
Bucephalus	65
Son Of the Soil	66
Borneo Mask In Flea Market	67
When I Woke Up	68
Tryptych, Trilingual	69
From a Sea-View Balcony	71
Purple Orchid	72

Driving To a Neighbourhood Supermarket   73
Houses   74
Watermelon Juice   79
Godeshwaram Beach   80
Common Objects   81
Curry Leaves   83
Seashell   84

About The Author   85

Leaves

Double bind of my soul
warped in time's distending shadows;
dead leaves dressing the earth
hide a remote warmth calling
through visceral aches, across ancient fields.
I slow down these mysteries
surrounding me this day,
bits and pieces of wonder stuck here
in these crevices, these woods,
these last outposts of where I belong.
A dragon fly's skeleton floats,
a silent fossil inspecting the pond's stillness
this reservoir of weeds
and magical fables narrating green.
I slow myself down
letting the oriole cry into my voice
letting crickets explain
unsaid compromises, shadows of past.
Dead leaves don't rustle here anymore;
no one keeps a chronicle of events
and sudden unfolding of sunlight's surprises.
When light came
they found me become one with those leaves.

Shadow That Became Rains

In twitching despair
eyes became a mutiny of fireflies
burning the night.
The skull was a hollow prison
from which the wind escaped.
Hair was moss
arising from the earth's scalp;
teeth turned into barricades
that kept his words out
of nightmare's search.
Fingers melted into woods
bones into ashes
nails bloomed into globe amaranth
his voice became
a meteor's last hissing fall.
Legs grew roots
seeking the soil's wetness,
veins were green nets of chlorophyll,
blood flowed into mandhara flowers.
His name became one
with the hamlet's
with whom he shared this night.
When his body switched on the lights
its shadow had become rains
knocking on the tile roof
struggling to be let in.

Witnessing Creation

I was there
in the motherland
of first lightning
and crimson noons
and carbon soup
where rocks melted
in an inchoate ocean of rage
that did not stir.
I happened to be there
reclining like a sea snake
discerning an accident
inhabiting that bubble
before it burst
like a prism's clairvoyance.
I split the first light
and lived a life
without shadows;
no symmetry,
all tangled geometry.
There was I
not even a body
floating like vapour
touching stars
splintered as shards into the soil.
Language seemed improbable
in that thunder,
divisions couldn't be conceived;
it was plasma
hot orange to touch
stinging your flesh.
I floated in a cockpit of dreams
and saw an ice-moon flickering.
Before I knew
sparks and lava-roses

continued

ignited a double helix in me.
The planet had to be named
and with that I became several –
standing in
for all that I sought
to understand.
I remain to this day,
the word.

Face On Mirror

I brushed the glazed façade
that looked into me mournfully -
eye for an eye;
the lustre I perceive lets my universe
into a dressing table's vanity.
Behind the mirror
are deceptions, a self
tricking itself, pretending that flesh
has hidden the dismay
inside skull's reptilian grotto –
figments,
reflections of our brief survival
as men set free beyond their bidding.
There is thunder outside and lightning
that braves new moon darkness, it is clear
that 'grandfather's beards' have floated
and disappeared with the clouds
into the evening's lingering unease.
Only silence can sum up this impreciseness
as clusters of light settle on silvery smoothness
and we look into our less than tranquil faces
busily contorting a profound fear.
The mirror has its moments of clarity too
when the fear it creates in us
retrieves a lost impulse, integrity
of appearance not judged by the world,
and its mundane irrelevance.
Between the face's aloneness
and its unflattering image
we inspect the mirror –
eye for an eye –
perplexed
and alone.

I Dreamt Of Grandfather Last Night

Indifferent meteors
traveling with dreams
light candles for midnight's vigil.

I open a gently shut teak door
and enter a courtyard smelling of ripe mangoes.
Bats, a hungry cohort
of what it means to be blind in day's best hours
are waiting,
more dense than darkness
on those branches.
I merely ignore their eyes
as they size my presence upside down

I pass the Thulasi plant,
and the dog's barking
stopping my thoughts
running away with this night's complicity.

It was then that I saw him
clearly as in first light,
lying placidly on his easy chair,
a frail, weakening intelligence
draped in starched cotton mundu
and tired ribs
simply staring at me, and beyond,
his jaws frozen in time
in deepset bemused paralysis.

I dreamt of my grandfather last night.

Time's Prisoner

A word's sinking sediment of meaning
hides in this forest of light
now trickling into my neurons;
now firing, slow heat
after an unusual evening snooze.
Time is delinquent:
imprisoned in discipline's regimen
of things to do this day.
I have hit modernity's
repose of unsettling trivia
dancing on disco floors,
an angel born from
the idiot's picture tube
and strobe lights,
a blob of visual plasma
surrounding my senses.

A word uttered — the remainder
after sediments disappeared
into my ocean of consciousness -
stares at me expecting comprehension.
It has come from
an obedient gene's
doublespeak of spiral helix
that must have drowned me
inside my mother's womb.
It may be a great grandmother's
complaint or a myth
she narrated in profound sadness.

Clouds have entered
grey zone of rains
and surreal daydreams.
They will soon whip
this hamlet's dry humour

continued

of summer dust and empty fields.
A hydraulic crane watches
a miracle of birth
becoming water
from still heights.

Rules remembered
strode into my vision,
a steely contraption
strung together
by meek language
and flux.
A man has denounced
his shadow again
in the name of religion,
wicked faith
sitting with perverse skeletons
in Giger,
a steel skeleton without testicles.

What evolves next?
A pigeon appears as devil
brooding on my parapet
preening in sunlight.
A touch on my hand
was meant to appease
my godlessness, and
a morality not bound
by creation's impasse.
Grammar tugs me,
a kind grammar
taught to me in school,
an old fashioned school
devoid of poetic license.
This is the second day
after a mudslide crushed

Philippinos, in the rushed calculus
of weather forecasts gone awry.
This is an evening of stillness,
of grief, of remembered rules
returning to my attention.

I sit below a tamarind tree
of surprises:
a squirrel devoted to rummaging
fondness stops to reminisce
on its branches,
around a bunch of sourness
a kingfisher
plans his next dive
into a nearby pond's ancient depths,
a cow tethered
to its trunk
has become a benign
trace of cow dung
and bovine memory.

I have become one
with this flesh of sourness,
a sentinel guarding
the pale sky's retinue
of invisible ancestors.

Sadness, my companion,
has disappeared into the twilight mist.

Tamarind Tree

Dissect the freckled shade that tunes
the frequency of this cloudy afternoon,
and I will appear –
an unkempt ancestor of your language
of leafy words and unripe grammar.
You make me feel I belong
to your forest of lies, now awaiting
rains and mercy
in this confined valley of sadness.
I stand, like a forlorn soldier
from a movie, my world
a grey ghost-country ridden with doubt's bullets:
Will I shed my leaves in time
for the infant girl to pick up
on her way to the funeral?
Will the returning painter, that man
who abandoned his name, recognize
scars that his palette introduced
on my history of darkening hide?
You say you are a poet, seeking
silence instead of pauses in your rhythms.
I say you are a poet, only
because my leaves and fruits remind you
of exclamation marks, wonders,
goats grazing self-assuredly
and colours of marigold petals.
The sourness I convey behind my rind
is the only poetry I taught you,
a wooden heart's clambering pleasure.

Walking To the Duck Pond

Beyond my ancestral tug
stepping out into wide open paddy fields
along a cool slush
of rain-swept granite-edged canal,
two frail old women scurry
with baskets of paddy husk
and burden on their heads.
Their eyes dislodge colours
packed into this sunshine and monsoon's fertile touch,
ignore bone's wear and bored tear,
configure muddy rectangles
of green beside memories.
Beyond them
a few sodden footprints
and mukkutti blooms
snared in this field's smothering crowd
of stalks and insects in toad territory.
And a path that ends
in a duck pond, as if surprised.
The sun is stretched
into this pond, and its fire
has turned a soft green
reflected from this water
and arguably, celestial envy.
You ignore sun's pond-smoothened hue
a habit born from fear of eclipses
and primal reflex,
like reptilian revulsion.
On the pond, banyan tree leaves
and what remains after duck's courtship,
ripples, feathers and other sulking birds.
You remain in this banyan tree's shade
fraught with daydreams and prospect of rain.
The two old women have disappeared, white clouds
swallowed by hillocks a hundred yards away,

continued

clouds waiting to talk to earth's dryness
and prayers of farmers snared by these paddy fields.
You sense this afternoon is crowded.
It is waiting to erupt
with voices snared by these paddy fields.
As clouds gather, mynahs hiding in these fields
adjust the urgency of their mating calls;
only banyan leaves clasping the pond's unguent textured
ripples remind you of your aloneness.
Quietness and disappearing grandmothers
cannot conceal facts:
this afternoon is crowded,
waiting to erupt.
I remain under cover of banyan tree
waiting to erupt, to talk to earth's dryness
I remain clasping my aloneness
with ducks snared on this pond's surface
waiting to erupt
as loud courtship calls
waiting to erupt as rains
snared in these paddy fields
biting into these unguent textured ripples and dents
rains fraught with daydreams
waiting to erupt on this pond with thunder.

Flame-Of-the-Forest, Beypore

Resolute, this air's coolness
is a tree outstretched
as billowing brittle branches.
Tree-prints stand
on a glazed plate of blue
and dampness in this two-dimensional
province carved from illusion
and scent of coconut trees.
These trees in robust tender alertness,
they are murals set against many skies
created after rainbows,
our hunger for freedom held
into wood and angry red
blooming along a brick wall
flirting with crooked tar roads
and fisherman's route.
Wild grass touching our feet -
a passive ticklish resistance -
instill fear of venom
and much promise of mirth;
the quietness around us
is replete with legends
and elephant dung, threaded
into a story of accents
lent by crows fighting
for a right to inhabit our ancestry
and steal at will. Red waves of ample petals
dart through a wedge created by sun
with a broken branch's connivance, a slice of
sunshine broken away from dawn sky,
settling on Flame-of-the-forest as wasps,
stinging our solemn eyes.

continued

Words we desired in poetry
strung through our vision,
impaled smells.
They exploded - those scarlet petals
in robust tender alertness.

Moulded Vessels

Cupped hands of this night hold loneliness
in the guise of an island by the Arabian Sea.
Crabs devour emptiness,
sleep is a euphemism for their fears
dancing under the moon's rainbow.
Love is the fire and you, the moulded vessel.

Strokes of lightning ignore our shapes
crouching with hermit crabs
hiding beneath casuarina trees.
The murals you imagined
on the moon's pock-marked face
lend their colours to ashes from a dead star
smeared on the cremation ground that is the sky.
Their dreams become our slowly emerging vocabulary,
a series of Michel Angelo ruminations
under the dome of dark anxieties.
We yearn to sleep and stretch the meanings
of what our names mean, for home's warmth
and this fire's unmeasured heat, this love.
You wonder if thunder
is the clouded rage from within.
Birds flutter in our eyes
their feathers streaked with lightning's
incendiary fingers, the flames
ignoring our flesh – temples carved in stone
warm to affection's touch.
We feel the soft granite we slept on
as ducks waded in the pond
below the sagely banyan tree.

We lost our souls and regained them
and wait for that cycle again –
lightning, voices, fallen stars, fitful sleep,
lightning ignoring our flesh again,

continued

waiting for the fire to arise
amid these leaves, these twigs
assembled by the breeze.
I see my skin as thin as this water's film of mirages
connecting the tree to spider's deceit.

I feel the fire's embrace as we sink into its penumbra.

Love is the fire,
and we, the moulded vessels.

War Against Terror

History is waiting at the threshold
to reclaim all that our shadows put behind them
and the chill of the night digs into our heels
as dreams fall into the earth with shooting stars.
You are wearing hurt and sleepiness in your eyes,
a certain wistfulness that goes with this forest's voice
of crickets, and fog and ancient sadness. I am not
sure any more whether we belong to this night,
this coldness staking its claim on our thoughts,
our bones. You remind me of a vacant spot
in the greenery where predators sleep, dreaming
of their hind legs looking like fallen columns
among ruins of Hampi.
May the world we left behind
leading to this forest recuperate.
May this stillness prevail
over the crickets' cacophony.
The war against terror has just begun for us this night.

Tracing This City's Mythology

I discern a mythology
far away from where Brahminy kites
glide into our lives,
their flights, a detour
into arecanut trees by my bedroom window.
Look at this city's faded motifs.
A bird's eye-view is needed
to feel its pain etched into bylanes
arteries of steel, glassy facades,
smells, failings tugging like anchors.
I wish something here would talk to us
that these green patches hidden among people,
two-room homes and hoardings
would sense our awkwardness,
sense our sleepwalker's body language.
The morning newspaper does nothing to help
merely recoding another day has gone
into this misshapen earth's chanting into oblivion
far away from the Brahminy kites.
Another day has just walked into shadows.

Childhood

Where are the ants
that made the pond
their excuse for communion
and the chembu plant's skin
that survived the monsoon's
plea for wetness?
And the fallen parasite
cavorting with mud –
where has it buried
its instincts of survival?

Days were longer
than shadows born
from this sticky womb
of rain water and trapped sun,
and we stared –
my brother and I -
into the gaunt sky bitten
by may flies and woodpecker's grit.
I was a wisp of the morning;
my will, a cloud
that gathered folktales
flying through paala trees
was cornered by a sleepy cat
searching for its lost tail.
Cold eyes sized me up
before yielding to sleep
before standing up boldly to monsoons
before curling up into a predatory cotton ball
that my brother hurt with a jagged pebble.
We screamed
till our voices trailed away
as crows,
feathers retaining life through sheer sorcery.
Our screams rattled red ants,

continued

a convoy of miniature demons
studying clouds that were lured by earth's desire,
those fallacies we perceive as monsoon.

Somewhere, winds dragged
a nest to its untimely death
and we watched lives that could have been
disappear into earth as worms.
Where is that path of worms we traced
before rains concealed soil's dubious purpose?

The Ashoka tree was sick of its ageing lethargy
and bled flowers till the sky turned crimson
with vigour, and fear of ancient revenge
for an epic kidnapping.
My father's deities retreated into a remote
dilemma which we called clouds,
now courting a rainbow timidly.
I inhaled smell of mandara flowers
the smell sung a tune in my lungs -
sadness set to music -
the song became a pond
where small fishes swum like lyrics;
the song then became a heron
feeding on those fishes.
Where have the pauses
that clogged my lungs
during those songs been hidden?
Where is the porcelain jar
which contained those pickled smells?
Where is that bronzed heron
my brother startled in his dreams?
Where is the blood dripping from Ashoka trees?

And at night I saw stars
peeping through our bedroom window

forget their constellations
and join emeralds on my bedspread
to become placid coolness,
serene as dawns without breeze
or presence of crows.
Each star became a dewdrop
each dewdrop fed an embryo
each embryo became a translucent figment
that grew with the specter of my imagination.
I saw my brother gulp a star down
in his sleep-walk,
trundling through his descent
on our teak stairs with glowing throat,
unable to dull
that gaze to this age.
A few stars exploded
became the seven sages
became coriander leaves trapped in our courtyard
became sparks that froze into ice inside our bedroom mirror
became grins by early morning,
and morning hooked on to a comet
vanishing through the peephole of our thoughts
exiting from the known universe.
Red ants had dissolved into the sky,
with paala flowers, and dead stars.
Oh, how we discerned that comet's trail,
and mysteries of red ants beside the moon,
my brother holding the flash light
momentarily brightening lizard's eggs
tucked between soggy papaya leaves.

Where are the red ants, those tunes
that clogged my lungs, and dead stars
marching into bedroom mirrors?
Where is that comet's trail into oblivion?
Where are the brightened lizard eggs?

An Indian In Manhattan

Sounds that intrude. Alien smells. Glitter
of a chandelier trading its mirages
in the corridors of this old hotel.
Outside, a pale rain which has arrived
to nurse a tramp's festering wound.

This then is Manhattan's arrogance:
A city moored to movements and rudeness –
somehow distant from a horizon
wedged between two skyscrapers, in grey realms
which only immigrants can inhabit.

Do I walk in the city's underbelly now
as I respond to an uncertain traffic symbol -
a pulsing red palm stretched into this sunlight -
that affluent pedestrians in gray suits
around me seem to ignore?

A street artist peddles his water colour
creation on Lexington Avenue, a splashing
of crimson and green and yellow which coalesce
into this city bus, this sullen tree drooping
into St.Patrick's cathedral, this hastiness
of pedestrians around me. There is no representation
in his art; our worlds will not meet.
I do not see what he sees around me.
I can only discern a cold drizzle,
and gray suits, and a pillar of ghosts
holding elevators and a name.
A pulsing red hand
warns me: strangers remain strangers
in Manhattan. Clarity through this drizzle
that alerts me, like this city's rudeness.

Dip into its rusty smells. Feel the fear.
Speak to your memories of home.
Remember what they told you before
your jet-lagged entry into this cage
of centre-of-the-world angst and elegance:
"New York is a bit like Bombay, just more
cosmopolitan, more expensive, more chic,
more happening, more rude. And yes, the
cab drivers are mostly Indians". Across the street,
a plate of discarded doughnuts staring
from a black rubbish bin, a luggage shop
ambushed on its last lost-lease sale, a couple
searching for their souls in the sun.

Enter the Starbucks ahead of you, search for
a place to sit which you cannot find, feel
the immense relief of tangerine frappuccino
finding its way into your throat, now silenced
by the city's cacophony of ethnic voices
and financial bargains. "They can sell
anything here in America". The receipt
seems like an impulse which one regrets
in later life. $7.95. "How are you doing there?"

Tie your shoelaces wandering into this dust.
Watch the Chrysler Building erupt
from the concrete, like false pride,
like a forlorn sentinel.

Take in smells: coffee, residual rainwater
on the streets, a gray coat touched by cologne
and loneliness, the metal beside fresh paint on a coach.

Converse with your memories of home.
The pulsing red palm appears again.

continued

Forcefully into the sunlight – a group
of African tourists with loud guffaws
and peculiar waistcoats; they silence
the sounds of this street for a brief
restoration of man's induced order.

The long queues, the Latino ahead with
candy floss for his daughter tucked
beneath his arm, the teenagers
smooching wildly, the black guard shouting instructions:
I wait to enter the Empire State Building.
Humdrum of despair around us, frozen
footsteps of a herd, whitewashed wall
behind the ticket counter, a mildly glowing
incandescent light, a negroid voice
advertising itself as Tony, our virtual guide
through the maze of landmarks now visible
from the crowded terrace of the building.

I watch concrete slabs and ambitious monuments
scattered in this dark mist, now taking shape
as a foreground for the silvery Brooklyn bridge
foraying through the edges of water, this city's
lickspittle. A voice behind me, a burly father, instructs
his three year old daughter
to notice how the central park looks
like a Lego set from where we stand.
A ship anchored
in the still waters cries into the night,
a muted conversation
with this city that would
end in futile homesickness.

I converse with my memories of home,
alone in this crowded palette
of skin colours and fleshy mass.

Blackness clears away into golden
wonder beside my bedroom curtain;
the sun has announced another day
along with sirens and a lone shout
by the concierge trying to grab a taxi.
A bluish neon cross on the spire
of a granite cathedral holds out
the meaning of redemption
and the hangover of night's sins.
Lucidity is in the air, in the slow streets,
tinged with the imminent march of high decibels
after breakfast. Brief wafts of surviving
mist survey the empty roads washed
in the last rainfall, somebody's sorrow.
Through my looking glass I see this city
awaken from its comatose reprieve
into a play of moods and cantankerous
power games behind gray suits.

Soon, feet emerge, flailing flesh walking
on bony stilts adorned in Gucci and Armani,
proudly plodding through the dense footpath.
Clouds retreat into the sanctuary of blue,
the only cool presence in this hour.
The pulsing red palm appears,
below it, a tramp is woken up
by the shrill whistle of a cop.

I am in La Fontaine theatre.
Beauty and the Beast beckons
amid old-fashioned, trumpeting voices
and well-heeled patrons floating
into these aisles and leather seats.
A galaxy of tinsel punctuated
by violin sounds enter this grave

continued

hall of immaculate craftsmanship.
I feel a huge chandelier above
guarding the dome of illusions,
as sure as one senses a hovering
thunderstorm during melancholy dusk.
The frail music conductor
makes the final check on her
troupe. The fable is about
to be enacted, the archetype
of the beast's transformation
will unfold. The actors are clearing
their throats and conscience.
This is not just another stage
we see from a distance.
This is Broadway, where
fairy tales abound even in audiences;
I see a beastly presence in my row.

I converse with my memories of home.
The pulsing red palm appears
like a beast.

At Malibu Pub, Kuantan Beach

Corona of guile
moving as restless feet,
drunk in caprice
and bleak alcohol.

Is that my fear
laid on the table
with roasted peanuts?
My other side
waiting to become?

Outside, the South China Sea
has struck moonlight
on the white sands.
The crabs hear
the raucous whisper
of water,
a vulgar groan
rippling into night.

A wound opens
in somebody's heart.
We see them dance in glee,
those festering wounds,
to loud beats
dreaming aloud in this pub.

Why do men
retreat to this womb often?
Why does a tug in the chest
increase the air's heaviness
like a trauma's recall,
like a rank cigarette puff?

continued

A waitress drops
her hint, and a few
inches of her neckline.
Outside, a dead jellyfish
is washed ashore
from its smug comfort
and sinister home.
An entire world
twirls under strobe lights,
everything inches
towards instinct,
towards an island
of covetousness.

The hours move
through the smokescreen
and glint of earrings,
an irresolute advance
stumbling twice
before petite Chinese girls
can say 'yes' or carry
men on their frail shoulders.

"Its my life", the tune blares.
I see what poets
can see and celebrate;
loneliness etched into
worlds of smoke,
an uncertain distance from crowds,
an adamant clutch
on things precious to self,
a certain sadness,
a bridge we cannot cross
in this loudness, this heat;
a filth that makes
all virtue worthwhile for some

like an addiction of the flesh.
I remember the jellyfish
and its clotted
translucent tissue,
and a certain nausea
that accompanied the sight,
a visual epidemic.

Then it rained,
pelting the roses
on the resort's quadrangle
and the palm tree
dotting the swimming enclosure
where bare bodied tourists
made a pact with Narcissus.
We watched the rain dance
through the tinted glass,
hissing rains,
amid macho laughter
and needy band girls.
The slug that clung to
a rock on the shore
was fat, shiny, silvery,
like an angel from
tinsel town.

"Are pubs in Bombay
like this?", they ask me,
reminded suddenly
of Bollywood –
all those trees, and songs,
and pretty heroines.
"Sure. Pubs around the world
are the same for a teetotaler".

continued

The sea's breeze
pulls a raw nerve;
when I walked yesterday
on high tide's slender corridor
I felt the same sting,
the same sadness
one feels when sentences
become defectors of the spirit.
We laugh, three skeletons
filled up by light,
floating on bar stools.

"Cheers"…clink of
soul's mirrors, beer glass…
the seashells are attractive….
let the rains cease….
we are sure to find
jellyfish stranded on the shore.
The peace missing
from our vocabulary
was silence, sitting sullen
in a corner, sane, reproachful.

"Do introverts die
the same way as others?
Them with their fantasies
of after-life, unending
silences, enjoying every bit
of that drifting away from
the crowd, like the palm
sprout we saw, drifting away
from the shore's onlookers".
Refill for the two of them
as I watch self-consciously
at my orange juice receding away.

A sea urchin smeared with grime
is a witness to the sea's temptations.
Adjectives of the night –
gloom, isolation, longing -
are studded on a coral
lying on the sands;
they search for the right words,
careful not to breach
what their consciousness
would not permit.
Me, a curious observer
of their concealed motives.

Definitions

Surprise:
tiptoeing through darkness
the moustache emerged in the hall –
yoghurt on our daughter's face.

Quarrel:
it hurt badly,
those words that hissed last night
hooking skin-deep flesh.

Football field:
deserted green patch at nightfall
unsafe for timid, anxious lovers
before games begin.

Hibiscus:
sagging Cupid's arrow
pierced through red, velvety petals
entangled in pollen.

Pedantry:
what spoilt the children
when the rod was not spared
has to be impulse.

Greenhorn:
what was left in the park
after the poachers stripped off
the vegetarian's hide.

Petronas Twin towers:
mighty honeycomb
waxed into this city's eye
of steel and glass mirages.

Lost:
somewhere in these words and smells
that turn this street into a destination
I ask where am I?

The other:
beyond my body's odour
touching, talking, feeling,
reminding me of my own presence.

Sleep:
a tavern of dreams
threading forgotten silences
in night's vaulted beam.

Death:
the end.
period.

Drift Song

The wind that caught me
by surprise at leaf's brightest hour
when crows rummaged the sky for scent of monsoons
is a name freed from its body –
a spirit presiding over this wetness.
Frailties, remembered again
as I stepped into the wind's ghostly flight
have become sprouts of garba grass
and white madness on jasmine plants.
This is the pedestal from which
we survey our world of broken memories,
and aromas that bind me to my grandparents.
And the raindrops – how they slide through red tiles
to the waiting floor below, creating puddles
of bewilderment, teasing coldness.
This time I caught the wind by surprise
waiting for it at this afternoon' only spot
of warmth beside the well.
This, when at the leaf's brightest hour
a chrysalis conquered its apprehensions
as crows rummaged the sky for monsoons.

Bishop's Forest Trail

Cobbled stones sit
through slow lives of shadows
and slim rivulets born of rains,
tracing our path through this trail

of giant creepers and beehives
lost in damp heights.
I learn to decipher words
and aches of travellers before me

that created this cobbled stone path
and their unerring instinct
of destiny, and destination.
I conclude love is a habit

even in these ancient spaces
stopping to feel the bump on
our daughter's sleepy head,
now stirred by a crow pheasant's

invitation to play. Cicadas erupt
from silence, a hundred rashes
on our skins, stung by flies
and lack of instincts. Sweat

trickles down along teak trees,
an awkward resin that binds our souls
and the thinning cobbled stone path -
now like a shiny serpent of mud

and broken twigs lacerating fallen leaves.
These are first dwellings -
ancestral symbols, lacking pretensions.
We feel like symbols too,

continued

out of place in this intricate syntax
where rules hang as stubborn vines.
Halt! Your voice echoes
cadence of this forest. We halt

- flying foxes cross our path,
mocking our mastery of distances
and aerial combat. Fear hurtles us
farther into this trail, a primordial addiction
we must have inherited before
entering this green mould of absolute space
and abolished day-night cycles.
Where are the strangers in our lives –

mute banyan trees and curious predators?
Why do we hear only conversations
surrounding our fear? I conclude
love is a precaution, stopping to feel

our daughter's wail in sleep
and your breath, now ruffled
by the suggestion of a cobra's hiss,
a giant serpent of mud and apparitions.

Love is a habit too, born in this tent
of vague light, like fear, before we confronted
this intricate grammar of ruined sentences
uttered by cicadas and older addictions.

Halt!
Only, this time,
it is the forest speaking to us!

Lobby, Intercontinental Barclay Hotel, NY

An attitude of upholstered elegance,
glitz and old world waiting
for another guest's charm,
another well-heeled peevishness.
A black concierge, six feet tall,
returns to his bizarre grimace
at boots and strolleys rolling by.

I throw my skin's nowadays-not-so-unusual colour
into this mélange of cosmopolitan arrogance,
hurtling myself through the doorman's threshold
into Park Avenue. In the fading sunlight
I see the hotel, a silhouette lending sanity
to the anxious wait of an Indian cab driver
imprisoned inside his mobile, yellow livelihood.

He smiles knowingly; thinking of home?

The Avenue moves on,
strolleys and boots rolling by.

Ixora

No – it was not Ixora
but torches that blazed at night
spitting fireflies and smoke
that I met near the bungalow.
Not simple torches
but angry words that burned
menacingly, their apostrophes
and crosses twisted like sickles.
I watched a bunch of them hit
and sway in the gust;
not red tropical flowers
that they pretend to be.
They are my dreams walking
on brittle stilts, skeletons
that marched all the way
from my childhood, clothed
in blood without flesh
like bare truth.
Like poetry.

Near the Creek

A white mongrel
is swimming
in the muddy creek -
a scruffy dot of life
under vast black lies
emanating from the moon.
Between the cliffs
that separate our notions
and their rocky steepness
lies silence, a gift
we cannot examine tonight.
This is the river
of fantasy – a black sheet
of wonder - where my childhood
springs casual surprises,
unresolved covenants
which need more than recall,
and more than a touch
of this estuary's breeze to awaken.

Ghosts of kittens that wandered in our kitchen garden
are adorned in flesh here, beings that swim reluctantly
against these currents of silence.
We thought of beauty naturally, and our ancestors
who marked their presence in our thoughts
before leaving this humidity with migratory cranes.

A cloud is hobbling
on the moon's trail,
searching,
searching for a speck,
an illusion of whiteness.

continued

I cannot deny the temptation
to condense my thoughts into a speck,
a compact bundle of vapours.

That is how I entered
this muddy creek,
these currents of cold silence.

Playing With Wind-Goddess

As you whispered coolness into my ears,
through smell of mist and morning grass,
your journey became a mild reminder
of the day's narrative of wonders.
An intrepid explorer of damp nooks
and treasures hidden among bamboo trees,
you grew up in clouds hovering
around my hungry imagination. A simple touch
from you could turn my shadows into mirth
and rustling mango leaves
sketching alphabets on sand.
Your sights were set on what lay beyond
the grasp of this soft, red soil
and the boundaries etched by hillocks
a few furlongs away; beyond - into the land
where peacock feathers concealed by papyrus
awaken as fully grown birds.
It was my first tryst with magic
that remains as unconscious hope.

I was open to the coolness
and suggestions of virtue,
to values held like fluid colours
on a shifting paradise of flowers outside,
a bee-ridden bed of marigold, amaranth and rose.
I was open to the beyond,
to peacock feathers transforming
into human possibilities
and dancing birds,
to the twirl of several wavelengths
floating as summer heat.
A white cat that licked its food clean,
a smug embodiment of worldly wisdom,
retreated into centuries' old darkness
woven above earth's fragrance

continued

arrested in my ancestral house's tiles.
A wicker lamp stranded on a window sill
took over a stack of sunlight
rushing through the day's slits.
The cat was a genie,
nursing its coat in that dazzling light,
that I longed to touch.
Do you remember
I was open to the warmth of that cat's smugness
and the lamp's greedy assertion of sunlight?

Saltiness on my dry lips and howl
of your voice and shade of the mango tree
reappear - a series of minor, crawling events
building transience while I collected
fables strewn by grandmother
with rice grains on dung-covered ground.

Eye

I am an accursed
white bag of coarse fluid.
My fragile inch
bridging world and retina
is a taut slice of history:
an army of nerves
and hope fighting
impulse to look away.
Age weakens me
with foresight and sly
darkening circles of innocence;
age removes magic
kindling Spartan oddity.
I paint scenarios
scratched with fallen eyelashes
and lose hold on outlines
of matter, common truths.
I am colours
etched into striated flesh
waiting behind language of sight
and translated worlds.
I become sights I see, subject
and imprecise object.
Eyes see, therefore, I am.

Dialogue

Ocean's whisper
and silvery foam on our feet.

Our daughter imitating
cry of gulls.
Salty-lipped,
burden of breeze
on our shoulders,
we see the sun
clawing into this water's skin.
A dolphin's grey smoothness
lollipops into a crimson sky
and draws playful
orbits of mammalian life.
We sense each other
imagine depths
of salt-spray and
spliced sunlight.
Boats trapped with sardines
bring first hints
of forays away from shore:
a caravan
of floating wooden veils
steered by wiry men
who look like cloth puppets,
shivering in pale flesh
and bright lungis.

You clutch our daughter tightly
as the ocean reaches out
to touch her, now straddled
between us on that solitary rock
hanging into a blue, liquid earth.

We are waiting for tide
and time which waits for none
after crimson
devours a patch of our sight.
We are waiting for salt
to disclose its vast sweetness.

Psychoanalyst

Trouble began after this metaphor
arrived with evening's diffidence.
A petulant breeze
knocked on our door
to be let out. And a forgotten language
from the past tumbled
into twilight bleakness
graceful as a cat.
This was a different dialect
that none spoke -
not one of his personas -
a foreigner's sign language
meandering through his streams
of consciousness.
"Doctor, is this my eye,
the source of visions?",
was his question.
All the colours he named
seemed to be his eye's creation:
the purple of the parrot
that cleansed its beak
till stars reflected its flight,
the green of the mahogany table
that etched the borders
of our senses,
the elephant's red
that stared at us
from an ivory tower,
the beetroot's yellow.
The lexicon of rainbows
and the prism's laws
could not contain
the riot running in his soul

and we smoked silently
till whorls of delusions
leaving our lungs
explored darkness
settling on my couch's shadow.
"And what about my ears,
do they hear the stories
floating in this air,
as clearly as that train's
chanting from a distance?"
"And my nose,
does it catch the smell
of heavens coming down
to this earth, and the smell
of nectars smeared on clouds?"
"And my tongue, doctor?"
The tongue – a snake lashing
with venom, its forked grammar
and coiled flesh searching
for earth's coolness,
away from people,
away from speech
and sunlight's harsh truths.

"And my skin?"

"And my sixth sense
which tells me
you have classified my illness….
what about my sixth sense,
doctor, is that unreliable as well?"

The breeze that went out
wanted to come in,
and the language

continued

had begun to compose
a music of its own,
something which sounded
like jingle bells
minus happiness.

Word From Kingfisher

Kingfisher dives into night's
unending void, returning with sadness
balanced on his beak.
Sadness strung with weeds
from the pond's secretive green.
He must have felt the coolness,
the rush of water against veins,
the tranquil descent into submission,
seeing the night sky through fish-eye lens
a tin sheet breaking open the waters.

The pond was his inheritance,
my grandfather's property,
and mine for the records
in the municipal office.

The pond seemed greener to me,
a few seas away;
the kingfisher must be a diviner
quick to discovery
gentle to water's touch.

Miles away, at Kuala Lumpur,
I still hear the kingfisher
plummet from my balcony.

Metamorphosis

I see this third-world tramp,
host of warts and irritability,
becoming a faceless drone
driving this city bus, metallic caterpillar,
into dreams of this Manhattan night.
We struggle to escape
this cocoon of light woven around us
by this caterpillar, driven by
this third-world tramp,
now a New York regular.

Exiting a Subway Station, 34th Street

A window ahead
born from hallucinogenic fear,
a glassy tear wall of graffiti
ripped from subway loneliness.
Through these I look
and find unraveled distances
hustling into yellow of cabs
and lip-sticked pedestrians.

Smoke hisses, a spurt of anger
through a lidded manhole
warning me about this city's
perennial rudeness. Loneliness
becomes an obese tramp, slowly
settling into a corner, taking
the sun down along with her.

Onset, At Kozhikode

Marvel as the shadow
of the frock folds into the light chasing
the silver web of dawn.
The curtains say
something different today –
perhaps, in a different dialect
that only the drugged moths understand.
Did I travel to a beach with white sand
last night, and remember the leper's song
wafting into the groan of the ocean,
and the calmness on the face
of the moonless sky?
There is someone buried
in an asylum on the streets
overlooking the casuarina trees
that dot the beach, someone who drifts
into the day like a fleeting mist
and tugs my frayed nerves
as we negotiate the blind curves
on the tomato omelette.
It is 7 a.m., the last outpost of REM sleep.
Where have I misplaced my dentures?
Where have I forgotten
my memories?
Where is the calmness
on the moonless sky?

Picking Yellow Beads

The truth has always
been suspended in clouds
above those limits
that this hamlet's hillocks built.

Not quite hanging there
like vapours, or hoping
for rain that washes down
some summer afternoons, but
just an eerie existence,
something like a flickering tongue
that you know can talk, but doesn't,
choosing to intimidate instead.

The inferences worked out through ages
of sleep lie on our feet now.
You see a shadow, and say the whip
of Indra is crackling in the monsoon,
and with it comes a lame duck's walk,
hurried shrubs, crushed twigs.

But, the truth does not matter
or hurt us intimately.
It is the waiting that must be watched –
the glide of the eagle
along the ridges of time
that defies gravity,
the belabored voyage of raindrops
into the earth's hunger.

Around the crest of the sun's
diffident reach in the sky,
is a cloud in limbo,
a white, headless animal.

continued

Tulavarsham, you exclaim.
Perched on it, a dreadful truth.

We retreat our senses
and wait for the answer
that evade us like rainfall,

silently watch the sky darken
the marigolds,
as we collect yellow beads
we picked long ago
in our grandmother's garden.

Silently, we watch
the horizon fill with truth.

Malacca

Lights on the night bridge
weeping pearls
vast straits beyond.

The Portuguese came here
with their ships
and brought with them
beards and storms.
It was little William
who became immortal
whose tombstone sits cold
among the fallen bricks
of St. Paul's cathedral.

"If you can stand
the smell of durian", she mumbled
against the tiresome groan of the sea
with a faint hint of finality
her voice trailing as the breeze
wafting into the colonial pavements.

Everywhere I turned
I found scents of broken history
souvenirs for the soul
postcards of paradise.
The watchman at hotel Equitorial
regaled us with stories
of Malays butchered
by the sea, possessed,
only to be traced
by the scavenger birds.

At the hypermarket
on the glassy road
a Muslim girl unveils

continued

the taste of McDonald's,
a steel miniature of the twin towers
reflect the distances beyond
this coastal night.
From my balcony
I see the sun
sink its teeth
into the flesh of Malacca.
Turquoise blue clouds remain
my last memory of the day.

Changing Colours At Dawn (Fraser's Hill)

Hills run into furrows
made by beliefs, outliving
scrutiny of deodar trees.
A momentary irritation flickers
as distant lantern light
and transforms into grey rock, lucid
resistance to my daydreams.
Thunder has ripped the bones
of a scarecrow about to smile.
Its toes are scratches in mud.
Hummingbirds that drew near
to my disquiet yesterday
when I sat on a broken toy seahorse
at the children's park
have migrated as disembodied voices
into the orang-asli villages afar.
It is under this quiet duress
of waiting that colours change,
crimson against my glazed fury of sky
dawning into awareness of fern leaf,
boiling coffee in kettle
and dim, prolonging shadows.
A winding road that disappeared into darkness
has returned, a patch of globe amaranth
severing gentle wind to pieces.
Squirrels scamper, chasing their aloneness
prying on lonely grasshoppers.
I watch the earth talk
with crickets to the unborn day,
eavesdropping on an ancient conversation
of bird's waking, dewdrops
and anxieties that attack my skin
like cold rush of water, like red ants
hurrying away from failing night.
I suspect it is a lion-faced monkey

continued

who weeps ceaselessly now;
only a cricket's cry returns as its echo
through the sun splattered canopy.
Colours change
into identities,
and my wakefulness
becomes a shade of red
flying away from this balcony,
as assuredly as a macaw's feathers.

Bucephalus

Steed that rode into mystery
and pain of Hindu Kush. You carried
with you pride and burden
of rugged pass, watched
acts of genocide and charming cities
raped to delight annals of history.
You carried Achilles' fears
and his untamed alter-ego,
your weather-beaten heels
scanning unknown worlds
of distant gods, Persian doctrines.
Nothing we invented after your death
carried our imaginations faster
or farther than your last neigh did at Hydaspes.
You tempt us with resolution
of a truth evading us.
Whisper from your tomb,
ox-head:
was your master a hero
riding with mountain winds
and Greek dreams?
Or, was he another savage genius,
one among several murderers
who visited our ancestral myths?

Son Of the Soil

Arches knit in eyebrow resilience
emerge among electric, massing clouds.
Thunder interrupts, a flash of craving
for earth's wetness and freshness
blanketing paddy fields. We carry a cup
of woes on our feet, a cage of brown flesh.
Flies swarm around us, hoping
for grains of charity, and afar
a rainbow is dismantled by an army of crows
scavenging the sky. Uncertain beauty
meets us. And bold transient strokes.
We have truly become sons of this soil,
settling in this primordial pull.

Borneo Mask In Flea Market

Numb is this wood's history
of chiselled face and carved nose,
rendition of displaced characters.
Eyes, tunnel to intruding winds
and essence of her lost tribe,
slit of unchanging hopelessness
and dimensions, peer into my bargaining eyes
in an outlandish language.
Which jungles adorn your gaze,
painted stare riveted between earrings?
The mask too is not in her mind,
lost among footsteps engraved on dust,
daydreaming about some wild fruit
that ripens in this day's straw-heaped
feel of dampness before golden axe
of twilight dismembers
this day's flesh painlessly.

When I Woke Up

I woke up late
saw crows frozen in white clouds
cunning black etched in white
saw winds laughing like demons
through spangled hills.
In my reverie, I must have bragged
about my youth, for the wind echoes:
"everyone is younger than a poet
with his countless dreams
tearing away from ancient sleep
lurking inside, behind arthritic joints
now painfully murmuring".
I woke up late
and became a few grey hair
walking on my flesh,
rudiments of truth
on my torso's scalp.

Tryptych, Trilingual

Among the banyan leaves that rustle
through this night's saltiness
I sense linear light, the theory
that condenses trivial memories
by footpaths, where I stop
to listen and then surrender my senses
to this casual coolness.
Three cardamom plants
talk their fragrance
like stunted forefathers;
three languages of smells and forgetfulness
that have seeped into my flesh,
intimate reflexes of my being.

There stands, beyond realms
inhabited by quirky clouds
and jet lag distances,
a small sediment of my past
stuck in red soil, ageing brick mansions
and anxieties that have deserted me.
Ponder distances winding through dreams
and landscapes scattered among common objects:
the lives afar subdued on my bookshelf,
a greeting card, aloof and foreboding,
my smallness on the saffron floor
cold as beads broken from the string
which held them captives.

The bills and eccentricities
of migration mount, silence,
and the aloneness of human life.
The quirky cloud
does not go across the sky
into the language of pain
and raindrops or water colour paintings.

continued

The blueness is glazed, devoid of peace,
a glazed shell of illusions
that roof our makeshift cells
of happiness. The seasons come
unannounced, another set of languages
that fold over one another until
one set of rules and grammar assert
and blossom into expression. They hang,
mantelpiece of the sky, spreading
arms of vapour, self-doubts. I draw
the circumference of my fragile presence
and see I have lost my mother tongue.

Outside, a cardamom plant has faded
into a surreal sunset.

From a Sea-View Balcony

In the gulf of time
a sea gull
loses its habit of flight
and white splendour.
Setting sun becomes
the only phrase
I mutter in tranquil
recall of absences:
home's wooden floor,
my daughter's touch,
smell of a messy kitchen
strewn with sliced onions
and soft, white-washed conversations.
The curtains of my mind
rustle with this breeze,
lifting to reveal a touchiness
magnified by distances,
and an interweaving
of images which is more real
than this smell of coffee,
this ring of telephone,
the absolute call of twilight.
I peel through colours
of this sky, riding nostalgia
of mauve to reach a deep crimson.
Outside, moon awaits
a charcoal-laden night,
seems to utter
tranquil recall of absences.

Purple Orchid

Does this purple conquer
green from which it is born,
loose skin drooping into this noon?
A barely concealed conceit
swells from its opiate lips.
Would we forego
sunset to watch it bloom
into stars, purple now
against this twilight's pull?

I am reminded of loss;
will this beauty
lead me to longing,
and puppet-play
of images, to flesh
I could have touched,
choosing to wander
in the path of an ascetic instead?
This beauty is sadness
barely concealed by dying light,
austerity's just reward.
I must find solitude
in this crowd of colours,
these shades of purple
now invading my world,
and my dreams,
these stars that carry sadness,
outgrowing the tug
of a green from which they are born.

Driving To a Neighbourhood Supermarket

We turn
into morning mist,
into an oriole's last moment
of daydreams.
Beside a rain-washed tar road
we watch our reflections
celebrate loneliness.
Sunlight has become branches
sinking into day's wetness.
Two kittens from a soiled home
come out and witness
parade of black tyres,
metal belching smoke,
and our Sunday drowsiness.
We turn
into this morning mist
into colours
about to go shopping
for rainbows.

Houses

Then, the breach
that divided a wall of light
from my birth
dissolved into cries,
flutter of wings I could not resist
as I lay with my eyes unopened.
That must have been the house
I was born in,
for I can smell Mother
and do not remember
its unformed memory
of tile-roofed calmness
and saffron brick floor
moist after parental footsteps.
It does not matter.
The first house,
I remember,
was built on shadows
and odour of elephants
that escaped from my imagination
reluctant to leave womb.
Sun's orange before milk-time
broke into a day's last breath,
settled on emerald branches,
disguised Ashoka flowers.
The tree met me again, a virile adult,
thirty years after outgrown shadows
became a real object severed
from my umbilical cord.
The neighbourhood has changed too
with bricks and new tenancy.
There are no shadows here
that take me into their arms.

A temple of recollections
and repose, living stones,
circled a well
inhabited by pigeons
invaded by banyan saplings
devouring its rough, red belly.
The well's green water was familiar,
as sure as day-night cycles,
a mirage of recollections
running deep into a few hundred feet
and my childhood.
Darkness resided in that cylinder
of green coolness, monsoon-traps
of sadness and rodents
and rare kraits
we found within its curling secrets.
That must have been
after I started talking
for I was alone
in that sunlit evening
throwing pebbles into ripples.
I even had a name
for stones that descended into that tunnel:
"Vellaarangallu"; its smooth texture
remains a living association
of my mother tongue's rolling affection.
Rain clouds gathered stories
scampering on rooftop
I was eager to hear.
In the soft rustle of running water
in a narrow lane which bridged my house
to world of men, I watched
those stories build up to a climax
of tender grass struggling to breathe
through white sand cocoons

continued

held together, by lickspittle gathered
around small granite stones.
Stones that gathered around my waiting.
They disappeared every day like genies,
the tender grass, bending
in a light drizzle
pattering on my mother's umbrella
and my chocolate-coloured school van.
They retreat to our home with Mother
while a wind whistled me into the school van
with smell of children, socks
and childhood leather.

White egrets tip-toe on green
weighed down by a bull frog's
incessant monsoon chants;
cicadas hum
into slow arrival of sunset.
Lengthening shadows of the monkey-god
flicker with the oil lamp; my mind
is caught between school work
and daydreams. Did the rain
hiss and knock on my window,
a slice of world fractured by wooden panes
and rusted metal,
through which I ponder
the vicissitudes of boyhood?

Ten
was the age
between the first breach,
the first sounds
and this pull of the window.
Each year
was a horde of shadows,
bright fables that lingered on,

surviving recall of that house
built on memories of rain,
tender grass, self-talk,
daydreams.

When we moved away
into a larger mansion
of shadows and greater width
girdled by real stones,
away from the red rapture
of Ashoka flowers and my birth,
rains came along with us,
but not the pebbles
or the stories scampering on the rooftop
or the monkey-god's lengthening shadows.
They stayed with the Ashoka,
old friends, fossils of my boyhood.
Why does the past knock on this window,
a distant city's glass,
scratching my vision with raindrops?

I woke up to smell of sardines
and fisherman's "kooo"
disturbing stillness of crows
watching Mother at work.
Dance of crimson
hosted by Rangoon creepers outside,
snake-like wooden resistance,
stubborn roots beyond a red-soiled verandah
in which we played cricket
and greeted old relatives.
That was the season
of pickled smells
and chameleons caught napping
beside the well's mossy parapet
and tongues bitten by dreams

continued

bleeding into mornings
while darkness pounded wetness
with slow lightning, and hormones,
heart's thundering search for life
and frivolous, failed imaginings.

World's crafted news
had just entered our house
in grayscale montages,
the idiot-box antenna
was a slithery creature of steel
standing on our rooftop.
From the bedroom, I watch
its spine dangling from a magical sky
gone awry in the invasion of monsoons.
I cry into awkward song of sunrise
and the large silence
waiting for this day.
A wooden staircase
and smell of white Paala flowers
brings me to earth below
and first meanings of day's routine
I cannot ignore.
Incense sticks. A quick bath.
The last smells of socks
and childhood leather.

Watermelon Juice

Fruit blood, frothing with longing,
lightly fomented taste or pasty remains
of what is left of fibrous, colonial hubris.
Melon of our myth, our casual youth,
enchanted fable's foreign pumpkin,
striped thirst condensed
into red meat of sweetness bracketed amid brittle seeds.
Where the tired river, Bharatapuzha,
abandons its flailing arms of shallow water
and abundant moss to flirt with April's tropical sun,
the melon arises,
a parable of planets and spheres winding through sands
of our white, sunlit memories. Near Bangalore, I found them
nodding by the highway chatting with sunflowers,
faintly gleaming docility
reminiscent of toothless witch doctors,
their stripes a white harder to reconcile with the banded greens,
a smoother visage of tempting touch
and masked clairvoyance. Myth; fruit blood;
enchanted fable's foreign pumpkin
feeding thirst of my soul, lightly
induced fomented taste. Remains of hubris in my throat,
voice of unguent sweetness, fruit blood.

Godeshwaram Beach

Sands, a crowd of still brightness
reaching out to stroke the Arabian Sea.
In the heat of one summer many had turned red,
blood of fishermen massacred by routine hatred
and Marxism's final turmoil. Today, they have become
the brightness I know them to be, the vividness
you reserve only for dreams, a trouble-free trace
of maritime history locked away in their recesses
yawning into this afternoon's halcyon lagoon
of mild ripples and haunted lighthouse
beyond this harbour's bend.

I am here after three years, a gratifying exile.
Only the fog horn is missing, perhaps
presence of the living too, the crows and ships.
The sharpness of their tiny edges
became a feast to my retina, a million bits and pieces
coalescing into delight, quaint hallucinogens
ground into this white earth's sodden belly.
Dolphins danced, clever intruders on my privacy
and the habit of blueness my eyes have adopted,
and at the stark rim of mortal distances
which combined the earth's fantasy with horizon

I imagined a kite searching, stunning prey,
scattering a few drops of red tinctured with sunset.
This was the land of brightness
where dreams met the shore of my exile;
halcyon blue of mild ripples and haunted lighthouse
becomes wave after restless wave of crimson waiting
tinctured by sunset, the vividness
you reserve only for dreams, and for exile.

Common Objects

It is a hairclip, plastic moth
glowing in a receding slowness
surviving between this day
and its eventual crimson death.
Hills staring through our window turn yellow
then add purple to their camouflage
distance themselves from light
and what must be conversation among clouds.
A bicycle left under a banyan tree
is a distraction, a black skeleton thinking
of its cooling metal soul and this hamlet's aloofness.
Hercules, it was called, this bicycle;
an ancient machine, it was said at school
as raindrops hissed at classrooms
bound by slate and teacher's dictum.
An enormous snail left a silvery trail
on corridors outside, wonders beyond reach
of classroom lessons, I remember.

It is my shadow, seeing itself
in a mirror's complicity and polish.
A thin, lengthening shadow afraid of flesh
and fragility of human life, a shadow
that wants to walk on pretending
there had been no glorious accident we call life.
The mirror sees a red sun
and my shadow merging with darkness,
fussy death accompanied
by flickering oil lamps
and hoary monsoon winds.
Crows watch, hordes of blackness
settling under banyan trees, and on Hercules.

continued

Sleep, settling down
as eyelids eager for dreams
and a home's silhouette outside
hosting a water lily pond
and mating calls of a bull frog.

Curry Leaves

It is raining.
A dark green sadness
and shadow of leaves
untouched by this wind's roughness
is my grandmother's memory.
A kettle announces
birth of aroma, and night
held alive by caffeine dreams.
Perhaps, footsteps
in the calm of morning
will remain as muddy footprints,
a souvenir, her last remembrance
looking at this monsoon
shaking curry leaves
by its shrubby shoulders,
its bark of heady aroma.
It is raining sadness
on the water's pimpled face in the well,
a dark green aromatic sadness
that will survive those shadows.

Seashell

The sea is rolling into this season,
waves of crabs
and ripples of disguised sunshine
that my daughter struggles to imprison in her palm.
A horizon for fishermen
and boundaries of our musings
etched into this sky's lantern peace.
Mangroves on the periphery
of sunset; a thin, quickening pulse
through our searching feet.

About The Author

Ajay Manissery Konchery spent his childhood and school years in Kozhikode, a coastal town in southwestern India.

His poems have appeared in publications such as *Orbis* (UK), *Blue Fifth Review, Indian Literature, The Little Magazine, Cerebration, Niederngasse, Kavya Bharati, Ygdrasil, Crimson Feet, Chandrabhaga, Brown Critique, Montreal Serai, Poetry Chain, Muse India, Kritya. in, Zone Magazine, Ampersand Poetry Journal, International Zeitschrift* and *In our Words: A generation defining itself.* He is the author of two books, *Facsimile of Beliefs* (Poetry) and *Drizzle of Yesteryears* (Short Story), and is currently working on a novel set in the rainforests of Borneo.

Ajay lives with his family in Kuala Lumpur.

www.ingramcontent.com/pod-product-compliance
Lightning Source LLC
Chambersburg PA
CBHW071026080526
44587CB00015B/2515